HELPING THE HOIHO

To my mother and father, who shared

with me their love of animals, plants,

and wilderness areas.

Written by Dean Schneider
Photography by Dean Schneider; Les Richards (stoat, page 11); Brian Enting (tiger in zoo, page 28)
Designed by Nicola Evans
Text read by Neville Peat and John Darby

00 99 98

10 9 8 7 6 5 4 3

Published by Shortland Publications Limited, 2B Cawley St, Ellerslie, Auckland, New Zealand.

Distributed in the United States of America by

a division of Reed Elsevier Inc.
500 Coventry Lane
Crystal Lake, IL 60014
800-822-8661

Distributed in Canada by

PRENTICE HALL GINN
1870 Birchmount Road
Scarborough
Ontario M1P 2J7

Printed through Bookbuilders Limited, Hong Kong

ISBN: 0-7901-0928-X

HELPING THE HOIHO

WRITTEN AND PHOTOGRAPHED
BY DEAN SCHNEIDER

I'll

always remember my first sight of the yellow-eyed penguin. Some farmers had told me there were penguins living near my home in rural Southland, New Zealand; so one afternoon I took a walk along the wild, rugged coast to find them.

I came over a hill, and there, sunning herself on a large rock, was a penguin. She had a pure white chest and a slate blue coat, but the most striking things about her were her yellow eyes and the yellow band of color which encircled her head like a golden crown.

I sat down quietly and, for the next few hours, was treated to the sight of many more penguins coming ashore, stretching, preening, and calling loudly to each other. Later, I discovered that the Maori name for the yellow-eyed penguin is *hoiho*, which means "noise shouter."

Shortly
after my introduction to the hoiho,
I met a scientist, John Darby, who was
conducting a study of the penguins. I helped
him with census work and his study of the birds. I
learned that there are only about 4,500 yellow-eyed
penguins left in the world, making it the rarest species of
penguin. Yellow-eyed penguins are found only in New
Zealand, living along the southeast coast of the South Island,
on Stewart Island, and farther south on some subantarctic
islands. I became so attached to these endearing birds that I
began photographing them on solo trips to the Southland coast
on weekends. I hoped to educate people about the
penguins' plight.

The drive to the penguins' nesting site could be quite
hair-raising. The roads were rutted, and became slippery
after rain. I got the car stuck so many times that I soon
learned to carry a shovel in the trunk. Mud splattered the
vehicle as it skidded from one side of the road to the
other. From the end of the road, I walked the last
few miles to the breeding area, with my
equipment in my backpack. The weather
could change from blue skies and
sunshine to rain, hail, and strong
winds all in the space
of an hour.

M y

first task at the breeding area was to erect a waterproof bird blind. This small enclosure would conceal my presence from the birds, allowing me to observe their normal, daily activities unnoticed. The hoiho are very shy, so most of my photographs were taken from the blind. I sat inside on a folding chair, with the camera on a tripod, and took photos through small windows cut in each "wall."

One of the things that makes the hoiho unique is its need for secluded nesting sites. Unlike other penguins, which nest close together in tightly knit groups, the hoiho are reclusive, preferring to nest out of sight of each other. A pair will build a simple nest in a sheltered place, such as a hollow log or the exposed roots of a tree. Here they have the privacy that they need for breeding.

For millions of years, the yellow-eyed penguins built their nests and bred peacefully in coastal forests, without any risk from land predators. But during the last 150 years, settlers introduced stoats, ferrets, dogs, and cats, which prey on the defenseless chicks. The extensive clearance of forest for farming also robbed the penguins of their secluded nesting sites. This has resulted in a dramatic decline in their population, so that their long-term presence on the mainland of New Zealand is now uncertain.

After the blind was up, out came the cans of cat food. Not to feed cats, but as bait for the stoats that I was trapping. I don't like killing any animals, but every stoat trapped was one fewer to threaten the lives of these peaceful penguins and other birds.

Inside

the blind, I read, wrote, and drank
cups of tea, waiting for the hoiho to return
to their nests after a day out foraging in the sea.
The first birds to return usually let out a single-note
call, as if asking, "Any other penguins around?"

Coming ashore can be a risky business for the penguins.
When the wind changes direction, the waves crash violently
on their landing rock. At these times, it's easy to
pick out the younger, inexperienced birds, as
they have a great deal of difficulty getting
their timing right, and repeatedly get
washed back out to sea.

One afternoon, I watched two penguins
swimming together in the rough sea.
Then one came ashore. The other bird
tried again and again to land, but was
constantly washed out by the high
waves. After some time, the first
bird reentered the water. The two
birds swam around for awhile,
before landing together
successfully. It was as if the first
bird had given a word of
encouragement to its
companion.

12

When penguins come ashore, the first thing they do is preen themselves. They use their bills like a comb to extract oil from a gland above the tail, then spread it over the rest of their plumage. This oil waterproofs their coat, and protects them from the chilly sea. Sometimes, when groups preen together, they bend and stretch in unison, looking like performing ballerinas or members of a low-impact aerobics class!

Usually the penguins ignored my bird blind. But once, a particularly inquisitive bird approached the blind and gazed straight up at me peering down from the small window. Still curious, he walked around to the back of the blind, where I was boiling water for tea on a small stove set on the ground. I didn't want the little fellow to get burned, so I quickly put my hand down by the stove. He turned, and nonchalantly waddled off down the rock.

August can be the noisiest time of the year, because the penguins start looking for their mates of the previous season. The breeding area reverberates with their shrill trills.

One day, I was sitting in the blind in front of a nesting site when a penguin approached the nest. A little later, it was joined by another. Some time later, a third penguin walked up and joined the pair. With raucous calls and a vigorous flapping of wings, the visitor was swiftly and unceremoniously pushed out of the area. At breeding time, two is company, and three is definitely a crowd!

The hoiho is a nonmigratory species, which means the adults usually remain in the same breeding area for life. These unique penguins live in two worlds – the sea during the day, where they catch their food; and coastal forest and shrub land during the night, where they make their nests. In the early morning, the birds go down to the water's edge and, as if in response to some private signal of their own, they dive together into the chilly waters of the southwest Pacific for another day's fishing.

The penguins' nesting sites may range inland up to one kilometer (two-thirds of a mile) from the sea. Every evening, they return to their nest sites, clambering over boulders, scrambling through bush, and winding their way across farmland. The grass can grow quite tall, but not on the penguin tracks, since they are used twice a day. If the track goes through dense bush, then it becomes a penguin tunnel, just high enough for the 65-centimeter (25-inch)-tall birds.

The hoiho lay two eggs, usually between mid-September and mid-October. The parents share the 43-day incubation period. The first six weeks after hatching is called the "guard stage." During this time, there is always one parent keeping an eye on the chicks.

The parents take turns going out fishing. In the early evening, the surrounding bush starts to fill with the calls of the returning penguins. The birds emerge from the overgrown track, and "run" up to their mates. The chicks get fed only once a day, but they must wait until their parents have welcomed each other. With flippers back and bills pointed to the sky, the parents sing a duet of trills and calls. Since hoiho can have the same mate for years, this noisy greeting is part of their pair-bonding.

At about six weeks, the two chicks are so large and demanding that both parents must go out to sea in search of food. The chicks are left alone at the nest for most of the day. This is called the "post-guard" stage.

During this stage, I set up the blind at another site, where there were some nests hidden in the bush behind me. Penguin chicks are generally fairly quiet during the day. Several times that afternoon, I heard soft "peep, peep, peep" calls in the bush, and thought perhaps there were two chicks. When I was able to peek, I saw a lone chick walking along a penguin path, calling "peep, peep, peep." Since it didn't have another chick to spend the day with, it was just "talking" to itself. So I decided to call it Peeper.

23

I n

January, the chicks begin molting.
Gradually, their fluffy, brown down falls out to
reveal the sleek, slate blue plumage and white breast
and belly. The chicks are then called juveniles
or, in human terms, teenagers. They look
like the adults, but without the yellow
eyes and yellow band around the head.
They do not get this coloring until
their second molt, at about 15
months of age.

After the chicks finish molting, it's
the adults' turn. It takes about
three weeks for the adults' old
feathers to fall out and be
replaced with a new set. Since
the birds lose their
waterproofing during this
annual molt, they must stay
on land, and are forced to
fast. They usually stand in
one place looking
dejected, and are soon
surrounded by a
carpet of feathers.

24

While I was photographing the hoiho, the Cousteau Society visited New Zealand to make some nature documentaries. I encouraged their land-based team to film the hoiho. It was exciting to be with this international crew. They filmed the coastal forest from their amphibian plane to show how logging operations and farming activities have eliminated most of the forest, the hoiho's traditional home.

By this time, I had become involved with conservation groups so I could be a voice for the hoiho. Extensive "Save the Hoiho" campaigns were launched, and fund-raising drives and television commercials introduced New Zealanders to the plight facing this little bird. As a result, all sorts of people, from children to business people, set to work helping the hoiho. Students, scientists, and farmers planted flax and trees to provide the shy penguin with shelter and privacy.

The hoiho are just one of many species that are at risk around the world. Soon there may be no cheetahs, pandas, white rhinos, California condors, or Siberian tigers left in the wild. These are just a few species in a long list of animals that one day may exist only behind bars in zoos.

We can all do something to help the world's endangered species, just as the hoiho are being helped. This can mean looking after the environment and not littering, polluting, or wasting valuable resources. We can help protect existing natural areas near our homes by picking up litter and planting trees and shrubs.

We can also support some of the hundreds of groups and organizations that are working to save endangered wildlife like the hoiho. It may seem like a small step; but if we all do our part, then together it will be a big step in the right direction.

GLOSSARY

bird blind – a camouflaged shelter used for observing bird life

bush - a forested area

census – the count of a population, often with various statistics noted

The Cousteau Society – an international organization that carries out marine research, and supports public awareness of environmental issues

endangered species – a species of living thing which is threatened with extinction

extinction – the total depletion of a species

fast – a period of time when no food is eaten

guard stage – the first six weeks after chicks hatch, when there is always one parent with the chicks

habitat – the place where an animal or plant lives

incubation period – the time spent sitting on eggs until chicks hatch

molting – the shedding of feathers in the process of renewing plumage

nonmigratory – remaining in the same area for life

pair-bonding – behavior between a pair of animals to ensure that they stay together as mates

plumage – a bird's feathers

post-guard stage – the time, at about six weeks of age, when parents start to leave the chicks alone while they go out fishing

preening – smoothing and cleaning feathers

reclusive – living in seclusion

stoat – a small mammal, closely related to the weasel